Using Energy

Editorial planning: Serpentine Editorial
Scientific consultant: Dr. J.J.M. Rowe

Designed by The R & B Partnership
Illustrator: David Anstey
Photographer: Peter Millard

Additional photographs:
Chris Fairclough Colour Library 7, 10, 11, 14, 18, 28;
The Hutchison Library 19, 26;
ZEFA 16-17, 24 (top);
Dennis Orchard/Bruce Coleman Limited 29;
M. Timothy O'Keefe/Bruce Coleman Limited 15;
Hughes Aircraft Company/Science Photo Library 27 (bottom).

Library of Congress Cataloging-in-Publication Data

Rowe, Julian.
    Using energy / by Julian Rowe and Molly Perham.
        p.   cm. — (First science)
    Includes index.
    ISBN 0-516-08140-3
    1. Power resources—Juvenile literature. [1. Power resources. 2. Power resources—
Experiments. 3. Experiments.] I. Perham, Molly. II. Title. III. Series: First science
(Chicago, Ill.)
    TJ163.23R69 1994
    621.042—dc20
                                                                                    94-13911
                                                                                        CIP
                                                                                         AC

1994 Childrens Press® Edition
© 1994 Watts Books, London

Using Energy

Julian Rowe
and Molly Perham

CHILDRENS PRESS®

CHICAGO

Contents

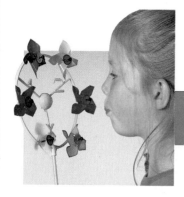

 SAFETY WARNING
Activities marked with this symbol require the presence
and help of an adult. Electric outlets are very dangerous.
Never touch a socket or the metal prongs of a plug.

Pedals and paddles

You use energy to move a bike forward
when you push on
the pedals.

You pull paddles through the water to move a canoe along.

Paddleboat race

Materials: Some empty matchboxes, used matches, small rubber bands, and scissors.

Wedge a matchstick in each side of a matchbox.

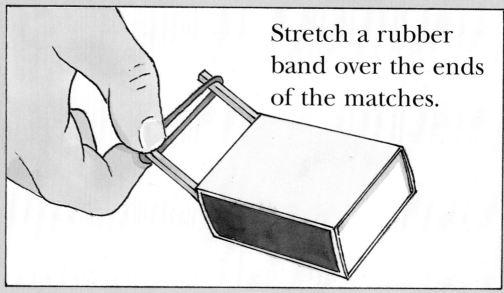

Stretch a rubber band over the ends of the matches.

Cut a paddle from the end of another matchbox. Put it between the strands of the rubber band.

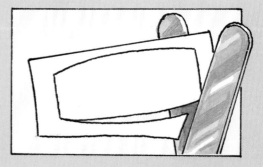

Make a paddleboat for each person in the race. When you are all ready, turn the paddles round and round to wind up the rubber bands.

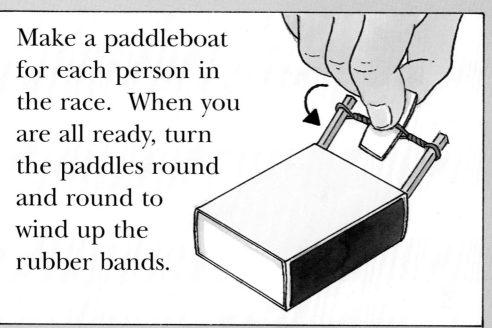

The twisted rubber bands provide the energy to push the boats through the water.

Put your paddleboats at one end of the bathtub and let them go.

Which one is the winner?

Water power

This waterwheel has small paddles, or blades. As the water pushes the blades, the wheel turns around.

The shaft at the center of the wheel drives machinery inside the millhouse.

Water falling from a great height
produces energy to make electricity.
This is called hydro-electric power.

A power station like this one produces
enough electricity to supply a large town.

Wind power

The sails of this toy windmill turn around
when the girl blows on them.
She is using energy to
make the sails spin.

Make a windmill

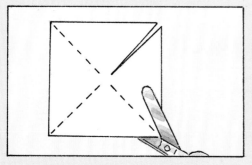

Materials: A sheet of paper, scissors, a pin, a bead, a cork, and a pencil.

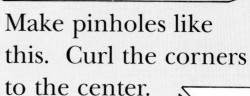

Fold the paper from corner to corner. Cut it like this.

Make pinholes like this. Curl the corners to the center.

Push the pin through the holes, then through the bead and into the cork. Push the pencil into the cork. See how fast you can make the windmill turn.

Windmills

The blades or sails of this windmill are turned by the wind. As the sails go around, the shaft at the center of the sails turns machinery inside the mill.

The machinery once was used to turn heavy stone wheels to grind corn.

Modern windmills have sails like
airplane propellers.

The sails spin around when the wind blows.

These wind turbines produce power to
turn a machine called a generator and
make electricity.

Making electricity

Electricity for our homes comes from a power station.

The generators in the power station use energy. They can use energy from coal and gas. Or they can use the energy of wind or moving water.

The heat from burning coal or gas turns water into steam that is used to drive the generators.

Electricity from the power station travels to our homes through thick wires, or cables.

These are sometimes carried across the countryside by tall metal towers called pylons.

Lighting up the dark

Imagine what it would be like if we had no lights.

How would you see to read in bed at night?

This city has thousands of lights.

It depends on electrical energy to make them work. With electricity, the darkest night is nearly as bright as day.

Electric machines

We depend on electricity to do many jobs around the house.

Electricity enters our home through a main line.

When a plug is pushed into a socket, electricity flows from the socket into the metal prongs of the plug. You can stop the electricity flowing by turning off the switch.

Many of the things you enjoy playing with use electricity. Others have batteries.

Batteries and switches

How many things do you have that use batteries? The battery in a flashlight provides electrical energy to light the bulb. A switch turns the flashlight on and off.

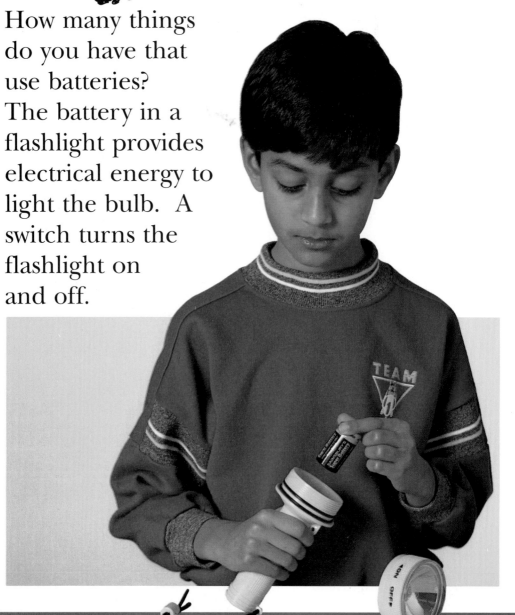

Make an electrical circuit

Materials: Two flashlight batteries, plastic-coated wire, a bulb socket and bulb, a small block of wood, a steel paper clip, masking tape, and two thumb tacks.

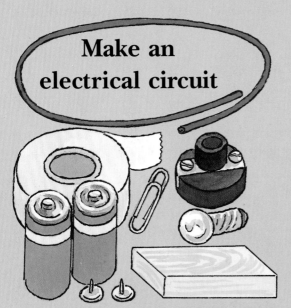

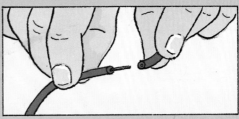

Cut the wire into four pieces. Ask an adult to cut off ⅓ inch of plastic at each end of the wires.

Make a switch using the block of wood, thumb tacks, and paper clip. Use wires to join the batteries, bulb socket, and switch.

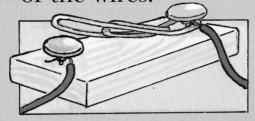

Press the switch to light the bulb.

23

Static electricity

In a thunderstorm, clouds become charged with static electricity. They can produce a powerful flash of lightning that contains huge amounts of electrical energy.

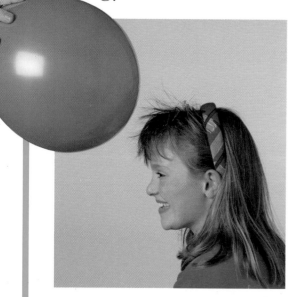

See what happens if you rub a balloon on your sweater and then hold the balloon above your head.

It makes your hair stand on end! The balloon is charged with static electricity.

Pulling and pushing

Materials: A plastic spoon, a plastic bottle, and a plastic toy duck.

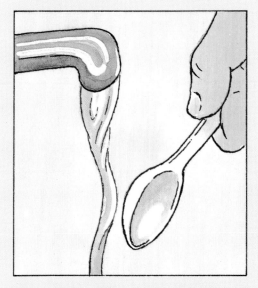

Rub the spoon on your sweater. Then hold it near a trickle of water. The static electricity on the spoon pulls the water toward it.

Put the toy duck in the bathtub. Rub the bottle on your sweater. Bring the bottle close to the duck. What happens?

What happens if you also rub the duck on your sweater?

Energy from the Sun

The sun beams out its energy to give us heat and light. This house has solar panels on the roof. They collect sunlight and use it to heat water.

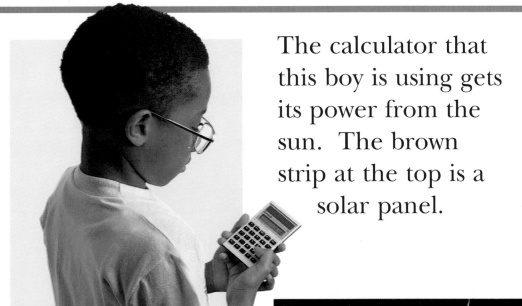

The calculator that this boy is using gets its power from the sun. The brown strip at the top is a solar panel.

Satellites orbiting far above the Earth also get their power from the sun.

Fossil fuels

The heat and light given off by the sun make it possible for plants and animals to live on Earth. Over millions of years, dead plants and animals turn into coal and oil. These are called fossil fuels.

Fossil fuels that store the sun's energy are used to make electricity. They also provide fuel for cars and planes.

Fossil fuels are being used up and must not be wasted. It is important to find new ways of using the energy from the sun, the wind, and the water.

Think about... energy

We get our energy from food. The energy stored in food is waiting to be used.

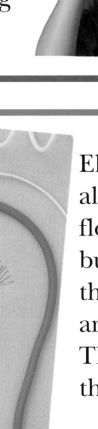

Electricity travels along wires. It flows through metal but not through the plastic coating around the wire. The plastic insulates the wire.

Rub a plastic comb on the sleeve of your sweater.
What happens when you put the comb near little pieces of paper?

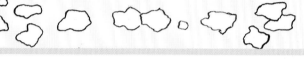

Before electric lighting was invented, people used candles to produce light.
What else did they use?

INDEX